# The Dopamine Journals

NOTES ON FINDING HOPE WHEN LIFE HANDS YOU
A NOT-YET CURABLE DISEASE

John P. Williams Jr.

To Carol,
and to our family.
Here's to our love,
our laughter and
our faith.

# Table of Contents

# Lace 'em up!

But then you already caught the idea from the cover picture of this book.

Lace 'em up is a call, a determination to run our race with:

. . . energy, not listlessness
. . . a forward look, not regression
. . . focus on the possible, not fatalism

So, get ready.

As we open up The Dopamine Journals, we are going to celebrate reasons for hope in the face of a recalcitrant disease like Parkinson's, for which medical science has not yet found a cure.

Underscore "not yet."

We are going to explore meaningful territory, like doubt and confusion.

We are going to be honest and investigative, even while we look for God's best possibilities.

We are going to reflect on the extraordinary difference that well-founded faith can make.

With laces snug and feet prepared to move us forward – even if we are dealing with a dopamine deficit or some other formidable difficulty – let's walk on, considering how best to navigate this race called life in an atmosphere punctuated by . . .

> . . . gratitude
> . . . hope
> . . . resiliency

What we are reaching for is nothing less than the grace to adapt, the will to persevere, a heart to enjoy the journey . . . and the good sense to recognize that we cannot do any of this purely in our own strength.

Ready or not, let's go!

# Journal Note #1:

# How in the world did this get started?

I never wanted to write a long book, but I have had the itch to write.

So, here goes a short book.

It's not a usual book actually; it is a series of journal entries that flowed out of my experience with Parkinson's Disease (PD) during the past five years or so. (Some of the notes were written in a regular, daily journal. Other notes were written in retrospect, journal style.)

This is a book that I never, in my wildest dreams, imagined writing.

Up to a few years ago.

Since then, as the reality of Parkinson's has rudely invaded my personal space, this has become a book that I could not, not write.

As I type these words, it is early 2017.

But let me go back.

It started with a twitch in my little finger, right hand, nearly six years ago.

It was a small, barely perceptible twitch at first. I figured it had to do with caffeine or the intense exercise I had just finished.

But it didn't go away. It grew more noticeable over the next months. And the twitch also seemed to team up with a bit of weakness in that same hand.

Six months passed and I began to have trouble turning over in bed, of all things. My walk slowed down, it even became a little harder to smile. I didn't like what was happening.

Who would?

But I kept pushing ahead in work and daily life, hoping it would all go away, like you get over a cold or a sore throat. It didn't, and I remember that certain night - about five years ago - when I woke up in the midst of an awkward attempt to turn over in bed, and I thought of my Great Grandfather Malone. He and Great Grandmother Malone founded what now has become Malone University. All through my growing up years, I had heard the stories about Great Grandpa's battle with Parkinson's Disease. He, of course, had dealt with PD in the 1920's and early 1930's before effective medicines and other treatments were available.

But that night, I remember thinking for the first time that I might have Parkinson's, and I recall blurting out a prayer something like, "Lord, I have always identified in many ways with my Great Grandfather Malone, but I never really wanted to identify this much!"

Shortly thereafter, I finally acknowledged that Carol was right: I needed to get checked out by our family doctor.

After running through several diagnostics, he told me that "It probably is Parkinson's, but I'd like you to see a neurologist - a specialist in movement disorders," and he gave me a name or two. (And by the way, "In the meantime, let's schedule you for an MRI, just to rule out a few other things.")

The MRI was normal, but it did require an excursion into the wonders of medically induced claustrophobia as I submitted to the massive machinery that hovered over me, just above my face for the eternity of 12-14 minutes, loud clanking sounds in the background. I learned that a little Xanax doesn't hurt at times like that.

The follow-up visit to the neurologist was memorable in two special ways: one, it didn't take him long, and two, he was realistic but upbeat.

I left with a new prescription, some simple instructions (including his admonition that "exercise will help"), a degree of disappointment (that "I've got it") but also a remarkable peace in my heart, a peace from the God who specializes in gracious interloping in times like this.

I recall running, not walking, to my car in the parking lot. I ran for one simple reason: not out of anger or desperate desire to get out of that place or an emotional reaction to my fresh and official diagnosis of an incurable movement disorder.

I ran because I could.

My PD notwithstanding, I could still run. So I did! With a burst of push-back freedom and stubborn protest.

From the doctor's parking lot, I headed straight to McDonalds for a medium caramel frappe and then home.

To Carol.

And that might have been the toughest stop of the day. She was so hoping that it was something other than Parkinson's - something transitory and curable.

As we talked and I bounced back and forth on the internet to fact-check our conversation and speculation, we held onto each other for dear life. At that moment, nothing on earth was more important than staying close to each other as we began, and I underscore began, to take new steps into unfamiliar and, by all accounts, somewhat hostile territory.

That's when my vision kicked in . . . but more about that in Journal Note #3.

# Journal Note #2:

# Since when is "dopamine" a big deal?

Dopamine becomes a big deal when you don't have enough of it in your brain, that's when!

Now I do not recall ever using the term "dopamine" in ordinary conversation during my first sixty-some years of life.

We may have touched on it in some biology class years ago, but the issue of dopamine was simply not on even my widest coverage radar.

Until about 5 years ago.

On that day in March, when my neurologist told me flat out, "Yes, you do have Parkinson's Disease," it was then, for the first time in my life that I began to comprehend just what a big deal dopamine is!

That's when I started taking notes.

My doctor explained - with the help of a few charts and scale models - that all of us humans have a mid-brain region that produces dopamine. It is called the substantia nigra. Parkinson's Disease is what happens when brain cells in that region begin to die in significant numbers, thus reducing the supply of dopamine in our brains.

Dopamine triggers our bodily movements - in our hands, our legs, in our jaws and tongue, vocal chords. Even our smile muscles.

PD makes it harder to walk, to write, to speak, to sing, to smile, to move. In its fundamental sense, PD is called "a movement disorder." When you begin to deal with PD, you start to comprehend just how foundational movement is to daily life.

On the psychological side, dopamine levels can also affect emotions, even joy and enthusiasm.

But I have to go now. It's time to take my dopamine replacement pill. It doesn't cure the problem but, thank God, it usually helps.

(If you want a full clinical explanation, you will find lots of detail on the mayoclinic.org website, for one.)

# Journal Note #3:

# What's faith got to do with it?

In a word . . . everything.

I am not into seeking secret visions and private dreams from God, based on the assumption that these are my entitlements, or that they are the necessary credentials for a "true believer."

However, against that backdrop of my wariness and low regard for high subjectivity, what I'm about to admit may sound strange: I, the cautious one, had a vision.

A vision. Can you believe that?

And it came to me fast, within minutes after I received the diagnosis of PD in my doctor's office, just as I was jogging out the front door toward my car.

In any case, the vision is "in" as they say in court, and here's what it looked like:

First I saw a stormy, angry ocean, --- right in front of me. Then, in the blink of an eye, I saw a lagoon, a sheltered inlet that was surrounded by huge palm trees swaying in the tropical breeze. At once, I moved away from the storm and into the warm and safe lagoon. I'm not sure if I walked or sailed into that beautiful, tropical refuge. But I know for sure that I felt safe and not fearful.

I cannot tell you whether my vision came from my own imagination or from God Himself. Perhaps it's both. But of this I am sure: God used this vivid scene to reinforce the truth of His love and mercy, and His multiple promises to reward our confidence in Him.

Hebrews 11:6 makes more sense than ever in this season of life:

> *"And without faith it is impossible to please God, because anyone who comes to him must believe that he exists and that he rewards those who earnestly seek him."*

Sometimes it helps me to get even more specific about my faith during this season of life. Like this:

1/ Lord, keep me from confusing caution and hard-hearted cynicism.
2/ I trust your promise of reward, however the specifics shake out.
3/ I have no interest in "fideism" – a disparaging of reason and the embrace of man-made faith in whatever makes us feel good.

4/ I am inexorably drawn to Jesus Christ - to his truth-fulness, his integrity, his power, his pure and personal love.

5/ You, Lord Jesus, more than merit my trust in you. It's truer to say that we are profoundly privileged to be invited by you!

So, what about that vision thing again? Here are a few take-aways:

With the vision came comfort and peace of mind. By the grace of God, I was not afraid! Unsure of how the future would shake out for me? For sure!

Concerned about how my PD would affect our family over time? You bet!

A great many more unanswered questions? Of course!

Moments of frustration and anxiety? Yes!

But not afraid.

(I came back to this Note #3 after I wrote it, because I need to add something: When I say that I am not afraid, it doesn't mean that I am the tough guy, the powerful, non-stop overcomer. It simply means that, despite rising and falling emotions, God continues to implant his peace in my core. It is his gift that I continue to welcome!)

# Journal Note #4:

# I get the facts, but there's more to the story

If you are looking for information about Parkinson's disease, it is accessible in abundance.

The day of my diagnosis, I hit the internet with intense purpose.

I soon discovered several resources which I am still consulting on a regular basis. Some of the best, up-to-date sites include the mayoclinic.org, the Michael J. Fox Foundation (michaeljfox.org) and the American Parkinson Disease Foundation (apdaparkinson. org)

Here are some of the phrases they used to describe PD:

> "It's not so much a death sentence as it is a
> life sentence."
> "You are more likely to die with it than from it."

And almost always the disclaimer coupled with the forward look:

"We are not sure what causes PD."

"But medical science is making significant progress in the treatment and epidemiology of PD."

Oh, did I mention that Parkinson's Disease is incurable?

Medically speaking.
As of today.
Despite intensive, continuing efforts to find a cure.

That kind of incurable.

And that hits you hard when you hear the word "incurable" in a sentence describing your personal condition. Up to that moment, "incurable" had always had to do with other people. It's a descriptor you want to shake off like a bad dream. But then you kiss your wife and hug your kids and grandkids; you take some time alone over a medium caramel frappe; you open your heart and your Bible; you sing along with Chris Tomlin, testifying musically to a deeper truth.

And you begin - slowly, slowly - to open new eyes.

I say these things not with superficial dismissiveness toward Parkinson's Disease, but rather as a quiet, personal testimony. I savored the depth of love Carol and I share in marriage and with our family; I lingered pensively over that frappe, glad for the flavor of life but uncertain about how tomorrow would taste; I wrestled with Scripture for a while and sang softly in the dark, at times skipping some of the words which seemed least plausible to me at that moment.

But I did land, ever so softly in a place where fact and faith are not at war and *"the peace of God, which transcends all understanding, will guard your hearts and your minds in Christ Jesus." (Philippians 4: 7)*

The Apostle Paul's letter to the Ephesians helps a lot, too, as I begin to grasp his visionary prayer in chapter 1: *"I pray also,* he said, *" that the eyes of your heart may be enlightened in order that you may know the hope to which he has called you . . . and his incomparably great power for us who believe. That power is like the working of his mighty strength which he exerted when he raised Christ from the dead and seated him at his right hand in the heavenly realms." (Ephesians 1: 18a,19-20)*

The Jesus who ran triumphantly out of his temporary tomb is the One who invites me (us) to run with him today.

OK, sometimes it's a walk, not a run.

But he promises life here and now, as well as there and then in heaven – a place totally devoid of disease and discouragement, the place of endless joy and insatiable worship.

Words fail. Descriptions pale, in our efforts to process his promises. And I am not in any hurry to leave this world.

But we can take heart with good reason.

Nonetheless, some PD clinicians suggest (even insist) that PD patients go through the Kubler-Ross five stages of grief (anger, denial, bargaining, depression and acceptance).

In my case. I have been blessed to spend most of my energy on what I can do about PD, rather than on what I cannot control. I chalk this up to the grace of God, my remarkably encouraging wife and family, intense exercise and good medical care – for starters.

And of course the stubborn symptoms of PD still remain active.

So buckle up. We are about to acknowledge in black and white several of the most common symptoms of PD early on. Our eyes of faith must not overlook the physical facts, even while looking to our hope beyond.

Take note that PD is idiosyncratic – symptoms vary greatly from one individual to another. The core of the disease, however, is slowed and more difficult movement due to diminished dopamine.

**Some early symptoms of PD may include:**

- cramped handwriting or other writing changes
- tremor, especially in finger, hand or foot
- uncontrollable movements during sleep.
- limb stiffness or slow movement (bradykinesia)
- voice changes
- rigid facial expression or masking.
- stooped posture.
  (A more complete list can be found on medical web sites like mayoclinic.org)

What a catalogue of delight! It rather reminds me of the long list of side-effects they rattle off on television medical commercials. Too much information in a short time.

I know what's on the PD list. I have known it ever since my diagnosis. I do not deny the reality represented by this compendium of possible symptoms.

But I try to put things into a more livable form than a cold list of possible symptoms could ever do. My thoughts go like this:

1/ For each of these symptoms, there is a growing body of knowledge to help us better understand and treat them.

2/ PD patients are finding relief and improvement through creative activities like ballroom dancing and non-contact boxing. No kidding.

3/ Anecdotal reports and scientific research both underscore the significant, even dramatic benefits of regular exercise, like walking briskly several days a week for 30-45 minutes. (More on this in Journal Note #8.).

4/ Like many others, I find the symptoms are usually manageable, especially when I focus on all that I can do, rather than what I cannot do. For me, PD makes it a bit more difficult to write, to type, to walk, to talk. " Nothing that affects daily life," as I said in a spirit of jocularity to my inquiring friend the other day.

# A few words regarding voice dictation

When PD makes it hard to type or write, I sometimes turn to the brave new world of computerized "voice dictation."

It is a good idea. A very good idea, this recent phenomenon called "voice dictation."

Here's how it is supposed to work:

1/ you activate the microphone on your cell phone or your laptop
2/ you speak into the machine in front of you
3/ to your delight and amazement, your phone or computer captures your spoken words and turns them into text on your screen ... almost immediately

The trouble is Joel is his nose work this week

The preceding sentence is an actual voice dictation which just popped up when I tried to say, "The trouble is, it doesn't always work this way."

Here's another gem, only possible through the wonders of voice dictation technology, just a moment ago: I need to go buy an interview things in his paragraph (voice dictation output)

What I actually said was, "I'll need to go back and edit a few things in this paragraph."

But maybe the worst experience I've ever had with voice dictation was when it heard my loud, unplanned sneeze and turned it into an uncomplimentary slang term for a woman, a word that rhymes with "witch."

I was horrified that the voice dictation software, supposedly under my control, created for the express purpose of making my life easier, had turned on me with such explicit and totally unintended trash talk.

Oh, and one more thing.

Do not, under any circumstance, send out your voice dictated message on email or by text UNLESS you have carefully reviewed and edited the message.

I never dreamed that you and I would have to censor our own computers and phones for spouting bad words under our by-line, but we do!

Accordingly and thankfully, the "witch" sound-alike that appeared on my screen never got into cyberspace, because I corrected the offending text before I hit the "send" key.

OK, so we've been warned that voice dictation can misrepresent our intended communication. Is there anything we can do to improve the accuracy and salvage the usefulness of this tool?

Yes! Absolutely.

Here are a few helps:

1/ find out where the microphone is located on your cell or computer, and try to speak directly into it
2/ speak slowly and distinctly
3/ be aware of background noises that may compete with your voice and try to dictate in a quieter environment
4/ dictate in short bursts so that you can edit as you go
5/ expect 10-20% inaccuracy in transcription, realizing that the software is getting better but still is not nearly as good a listener as the human ear
6/ compile a list – at least mentally – of words or sounds which are likely to be inaccurately transcribed by the voice dictation software, and either don't use them or plan to edit them quickly (I can promise you I don't sneeze into the microphone any more!)

Finally, here is the rest of the story for PD people like me.

It's another of those thoroughly entertaining, but pesky dilemmas.

It just so happens that when writing or typing get slowed and frustrated by PD, causing us to seek another means of communication – in this case, "voice dictation – we are still not "in the clear."

Why?

Because the PD that makes handwriting harder and typing tedious also makes it hard to speak "slowly and distinctly," per tip #2 above. Sometimes you feel like no matter which door you try, every door leads to a new species of frustration.

What I try to do in times like these is to play a little coping game in my mind.

I tell myself, "I am free for the moment of my smallish handwriting with its all-too-common illegibility; I am free for the moment from laborious typing on keys that depress too slowly under my fingers. So what if my voice dictation session gets 10 to 20% of my words wrong. I still win with 80 to 90% of my efforts.

It always helps me to practice enunciating.

And besides, some of the voice dictation errors can be downright bizarre!

# Journal Note #6:

# When people sincerely misunderstand

Regardless of how they express it, most people care about their friends who are dealing with some form of adversity. I have felt that many times from a whole host of people, some of whom I didn't even know.

None of us knows how to speak the perfect word all the time. Or any of the time, for that matter.

Secretly, we may fear that if we say too much about someone else's disease, we may somehow jinx ourselves into getting it. Come on, even if you're a Christian, this kind of superstition may have crossed your mind a time or two.

Or we may simply clam up because we are not sure whether our afflicted friend wants to talk about it. Or not.

Usually, less is more.

A smile. A hug. A pat on the shoulder. Or sports chit-chat over coffee.

Little things can convey a lot.

And when the time seems right for more substantial conversation, it makes good sense to listen more than chatter on.

PD folks are not on a mission to elicit frequent commentaries about their PD. In fact, a PD friend of mine recently told me that she stays home from social events sometimes simply because she does not want to answer the same questions again about her PD: "I wish they would just say hi and go on to other things, not my PD."

I get that. I'll bet you get that, too.

So, we might say it this way: "Don't suffocate me inside a narrow pocket of PD issues. Let's talk like friends who have verbal versatility and a range of shared interests - just like it was before my PD."

And, dear God, redeem us from over-sensitivity and the infliction of narrow exactitudes on others, demanding from them what we ignore in ourselves.

Now ... back to those "sincere misunderstandings." And there have been some dillies! Even as I write them, I am smiling. Not to make fun of anybody but to remind myself to keep a light touch on what can become way too heavy all too easily.

Here are four "sincere misunderstandings:" (with "malice toward none and charity towards all.")

#1  Upon hearing that I am walking and running a lot:
    "You're just like Forrest Gump"

   •   actually we are quite different. he was mildly retarded, at least socially; my latest intelligence metrics suggest I am not

- he ran for no reason in particular; I run for my life
- Forrest Gump ran in fiction only; for me running is as real as it gets

#2 One day, after a meeting, someone said to me something like this:

"Just repeat this after me: 'I do not have Parkinson's disease. I have the Lord in whom there is no disease of any kind.'"

- the last part is true
- the first part is denial
- the bottom line is I trust Him

#3 "Can you leave your dad alone for two or three hours or does he need someone with him all the time?"

- well-intentioned but a whopper
- Dad (and that's me) travels and writes and preaches and takes the grandkids to the play ground
- no worries about being alone any more than you would have

#4 "I hear what you say, but how are you . . . really?"

- doing well. At least, I thought I was doing well
- do I not look so good?
- just kidding. I do have to make some adjustments, but, thank God, I am great!

- how about you? Are those dark circles under your eyes? (kidding again. Can't resist being a little ornery)

And you know what else?

Thank you so much, friends of mine, for caring enough to interact. To talk. To try to make sense of the unknown. There is no such thing as PD without at least an occasional "awkward."

# Journal Note #7:

# Time travel in the anxiety zone

"Star Trek" made the notion of time travel popular and entertaining.

Essentially, "time travel" is the supposed action of traveling from the present into the past or the future. The most well known movie version of the phenomenon is "Back to the Future," starring Michael J. Fox.

It may sound strange, but when you are diagnosed with an incurable disease, your mind travels in time, almost involuntarily:

- your imagination leaps forward over the rest of your life on earth and lurches to a halt at your imagined last day, and that, my fellow mortal, is probably the first time you have actually personalized the meaning of the concept "incurable." It means the rest of your life
- conversely, your mind also flashes back to all those days and years, up to now, before you lived with any malady

that qualified as "incurable." And you feel a tinge or a shot or a wisp (depending on how you process) of loss.

Your marvelous immune system has, up to now, accomplished "full recovery" from every disease you have ever had: the flu, mumps, throat and sinus infections and more. And now, you've got something that will never go away in this life.

Anxieties creep into your soul, despite your best prayers and true faith.

You wonder what limitations you will face and how they will affect your family.

You don't want to think about it, but you do.

You begin to deal with things like fatigue and speaking difficulties and stubborn facial muscles that make it harder to smile. I felt robbed of things I'd always enjoyed. Things like high energy, preaching and teaching, spontaneous and warm interactions with lots of people. Every day.

But enough of the adverse effects.

Through all of this emotional, anxiety-laced time travel, I began searching for ways to cope and even more importantly, new ways to hope. I felt demeaned and diminished at times. I wondered what the Lord had in mind for me.

Then one day in real time, not time travel, I (again) came across the familiar story of Jesus' feeding the 5,000, recorded in John 6: 9-13:

> *"Here is a boy with five small barley loaves and two small fish, but how far will they go among so many?' Jesus said, 'Have the people sit*

*down.' There was plenty of grass in that place, and the men sat down, about five thousand of them. Jesus then took the loaves, gave thanks and distributed to those who were seated, as much as they wanted. He did the same with the fish.*

*When they had all had enough to eat, he said to his disciples, 'Gather the pieces that are left over. Let nothing be wasted.' So they gathered them and filled twelve baskets with the pieces of the five barley loaves left over by those who had eaten."*

Four things stood out to me:

One, Jesus cared deeply about people's needs. In this case, weariness and hunger. And, my soul testified, he still does.

Two, Jesus did not ask the boy to give what he did not have, only what he did have. Still true, I thought.

Three, Jesus multiplied his abundance out of that boy's scarcity because the boy released his grip on his tiny lunch.

And four, Jesus' demonstration of his power to multiply his abundance out of our scarcity included 12 disciples gathering up 12 baskets full of left-overs, one basket of overflow for each disciple to hold, to remember, to experience.

So I said to the Lord, "If I give you what I've got, will that be enough?"

And he said, almost audibly, "My son, that will be more than enough!"

"Really?"

"Yes, really. More than five thousand times, yes."

Now I admit that I still have some episodes of anxiety. But it's better. Much better when I give up my light lunch in deference to his multiplying touch that even produces left-overs.

And, thank God, although it's a bit harder, I still relish times of high energy, preaching and teaching and enjoyable interaction with people. Lots of people.

Just before we turn the page to Note #8, here are several "articles of faith" which, for me, make a huge difference in this whole matter of anxious time travel:

1/  God is sovereign. I trust him, worship him and love him with my whole being - "heart, soul, mind and strength."

2/  God can, if he chooses, heal any disease fast, including those which are deemed medically incurable.

3/  God does not reveal to us all the reasons why he does or does not choose to heal a disease here and now. Even for the Believer, there is mystery in affliction.

4/  God will heal every last disease in his eternity called heaven. In fact, the Bible promises us new bodies like Jesus' resurrected body. (Philippians 3: 21) How's that for perfect?

5/ Our God, whom we know in Jesus Christ, is ever and always the God of hope!

One of my all-time favorite verses from Scripture is Romans 15:13. It's about overflow:

> *"May the God of hope fill you with all joy and peace as you trust in him, so that you may overflow with hope by the power of the Holy Spirit."*

# Fighting back through the irony of exercise

Today, I'm thinking about "irony."

The word "irony" pops up fairly often in ordinary, daily conversation, and we have a vague sense that it refers to incongruity, mismatch - what happens when there is a great deal of difference between what we would expect and what actually occurs.

There's the irony of politics - when the fiscal conserveative squanders public funds; the ethics committee chair violates his own committee's ethical standards.

There's the irony of sports - "Can you believe the team that posted an all-time season record for victories lost every one of their playoff games!" Or the irony may be reversed: bad season, great playoffs.

There's frequent irony in child-rearing - "He was so courteous and conscientious as a child, but now as an adult, he's a twice convicted felon." Or the reverse: troubled childhood, flourishing adulthood.

And there is the ultimate, glorious irony of God's redemptive love: *"While we were still sinners, Christ [the sinless one] died for us." (Romans 5: 8 )*

Developing an eye, even more so, a heart for positive irony is part of finding hope in the midst of a hard-to-solve challenge, including an incurable disease.

It turns out that in the body of research into Parkinson's disease, there is a growing consensus that supports a highly positive irony: given that PD in its essence tends to inhibit our bodily movements, it comes as a pleasant surprise that regular, brisk bodily movement - yes exercise! - is one of the best ways to fight back against PD.

So doing the very thing that's hard to do - namely moving, exercising - has a healthy impact on the movement-inhibiting condition called PD.

I have to remind myself of this irony quite often; I have to repeat it out loud, because it so directly affects my daily life of walking, writing, talking, smiling - that sort of thing, that kind of movement.

And just because it can work so well, so beneficially, I would call the "Exercise - PD Connection" nothing short of a blessed irony!

This is a life-giving irony that I have attempted to explore and exploit over the past few years - since my diagnosis of PD.

I started off slowly, walking 30 miles the first month. At the time, 30 miles seemed like a lot. When I delivered the 30 mile report to my neurologist, I recall that he smiled and said, "I see you have started."

At that juncture, I had no idea how therapeutic and significant exercise would become in my life. But the more I learned about the benefits of exercise - for life in general, but more specifically, for PD in particular - the more motivated I became.

I considered all different types of exercise. Strangely enough, one of my early breakthroughs with exercise came about two years after my diagnosis. (Notice that for me, time has a new version of A.D.--- "After Diagnosis.") It was summertime, and Carol and I were teaching a VBS class for elementary school-aged boys. Given their level of kinetic energy, we made a habit of taking them outside to run off some of the excess. On about day two of that week, I set them up for relay races. As we ended our outdoor recess, one of our boys yelled a challenge to me: "Hey Dr. John. Race me. Race me." That drew another 3 or 4 boys into the mix, each of them repeating the challenge to me.

My immediate reaction (which I kept to myself ) was, "Remember, pal, you have Parkinson's . . . and that article you just read said, 'People with Parkinson's can't run or sing anymore.'" What happened next was joyful rebellion - against the article I had read, against my slower-moving, PD-plagued body and against all odds. I just took off running with our boys, all the way to the end of the parking lot. Running fast. Feeling the adrenalin. Laughing together. Proving to myself, at least for that moment, that what is not probable may still be possible.

I outran them all. Never mind that I was sore the next day. Or two. I could still run, and I decided I would sing again, too!

Now, let me interject a shot of reality: it's still hard to run; I don't push it or ignore signs of over-exertion. Probably 90% of my walk/run routine is walking.

But there is great joy in looking "No you can't" in the face and declaring, in consecrated rebellion, "Yes I can!"

That race in the parking lot started me in new directions. If God was going to give me grace to move intensively, despite my PD, I had better take up the offer and workout more consistently.

I decided to zero in on a walk/run regimen, starting with 2-3 miles per day, and working up from there with a goal of 4 miles a day. Some days, it's been hard to make my legs work that hard. Not enough dopamine flowing. Other days, I push beyond 4 miles when I am feeling the flow and getting that "second wind."

The best analogy I can give for the way PD affects my walking and sometimes running is this: you know how you feel when you try to walk fast in a swimming pool with water up to your waist? That's a little bit of how it can feel to walk briskly, given the PD phenomenon. Some days are easier than that. Occasional days are harder.

But how I thank God for the wherewithal to move and exercise, whatever the degree of difficulty!

On the practical side, I've tried to capture a few points that can help shape an exercise regimen:

1/ Be sure to get your doctor's approval before launching an exercise program.

2/ Remember: "I am not here to serve exercise, exercise is here to serve me."

3/ Start slowly and work up to an optimal routine gradually.

4/ The best kind of exercise is the exercise that I will actually do.

5/ Set goals and measure them; adjust them to workable levels for real life. (I use my Apple watch and "Pedometer++" on my smartphone to measure steps, distance, time, speed, heart rate and location. )

6/ Take it five minutes at a time; I try not to look at my pedometer or watch more than every 5 minutes. It keeps me focused on one segment at a time.

7/ Wear comfortable, non-restricting clothes and quality footwear; tie laces snugly so that feet do not slide around inside shoes; I also add a gel insole.

8/ Replace shoes regularly so they give good support. I replace my running shoes about every 2.5 million steps.

9/ Celebrate progress with people in your life who care (spouse, doctor, friend).

Since I started keeping careful records 2+ years ago, my goal was to walk/run the distance from home to Los Angeles, California (2,382 miles).

My actual results over the past 2+ years look like this:

| Time Period | Miles Walked/Run | Avg./Month |
|---|---|---|
| 26.16 months | 3018.45 miles | 115.55 miles |
| | | (as of today) |

That translates to 7,000,384 steps

My **current goal** is to achieve 4,000 total miles by this coming Thanksgiving, 2017.

# I can, I will, I am

The question is simply this: what do you do with your mind when you are walking 3,000 miles or more. At a modest rate of 3 miles per hour, that's 1,000 hours, mostly by yourself - which is exactly the point.

I like to celebrate the fact that the Father God who gave us his Son and his Spirit offers to walk with us, to live here and now in us.

Such a value proposition seems too good to be true, but here it is in full view:

When Moses faced a crisis of hope, he cried out to God,

> *"If your Presence does not go with us, do not send us up from here." In response, "... the Lord said to Moses, 'I will do the very thing you have asked, because I am pleased with you and know you by name.'"*
>
> *(Exodus 33: 15, 17)*

Just before that, the Lord had promised, *"I will personally go with you, Moses, and I will give you rest -- everything will be fine for you."* (Exodus 33: 14) NLT That's pretty clear. And that is powerful.

Often, while I am walking/running, I sing (mostly hum) and speak Scripture out loud. No, this doesn't make me super-spiritual or supercool. Or crazy. It's just my desire to try to stay in touch with the only One who can deliver on the promise to go with us - every single moment - freely giving us his love and what he calls "rest." (v. 14)

Do you know anyone else who can do that? I don't either.

We are, indeed, "fearfully and wonderfully" created with minds that are designed to receive, believe and apply the word of God.

When I am walking/running outdoors, my mind contemplates the seeming infinite stretch of blue sky at noon and the deep velvet shades on a clear night, radiant stars shining like diamonds in the sky.

OK, sometimes I don't look up. Sometimes I am just cold and I rush to hit the 4 mile goal and go home.

Sometimes, when it's hard to keep moving, I get absorbed in surviving the walk.

Forget the running for now.

But deep in my heart and clearly in my mind, I stand and walk and run in amazement at God's terrestrial creation and, more personally, his new creation of us as his forgiven, redeemed and reconciled friends. (2 Corinthians 5: 17-21)

Sometimes I just laugh out loud in this truth. Occasionally, I cry out in gladness. But always, I stand amazed in wonder and awe before him.

Some months ago, I zeroed in on six words that make a difference to me, motivationally and physically, as I walk and run.

**"I Can"**
**"I Will"**
**"I Am"**

They come from three treasure troves in Scripture.

*Philippians 4: 13: "For I can do everything through Christ, who gives me strength."* NLT

**"I CAN"** do all things - including today's 4 mile walk/run - through Christ.

Everything does not include foolish, selfish stuff, but rather . . .

- everything he calls me to do
- everything he wants me to do
- everything he empowers me to do
- everything that honors him

**"I WILL"** *Philippians 4: 4 - 7 "Rejoice in the Lord always, I will say again, rejoice. Let your gentleness be evident to all. The Lord is near. Do not be anxious about anything, but by prayer and petition, with thanksgiving, present your requests to God. And the peace of God, which transcends* *all understanding, will guard your hearts and your minds in Christ Jesus."*

- I will be glad in him
- I will seek his gentleness (strength under control)
- I will present my requests -- with thankfulness
- I will welcome his supernatural peace that guards our hearts and minds in Christ Jesus (and who better?).

**"I AM"** *Hebrews 12: 2-3 "Let us fix our eyes on Jesus, the author and perfecter of our faith, who for the joy set before him endured the cross, scorning its shame, and sat down at the right hand of the throne of God. Consider him who endured such opposition from sinful men, so that you will not grow weary and lose heart."*

- I am fixing my eyes on Jesus
- I am considering how much he gave to reach us
- I am sustained by him so that I do not lose heart

I must have spoken those six words hundreds of times over the past few years out of great gratitude and personal ratification. Never, I hope, out of slavish obligation or in the passivity of vain repetition.

A few simple principles have helped keep the six words fresh:

1/ I am not required to speak these six words and three Scriptures every single time that I go out for a walk/run.

2/ Nevertheless, I find it helpful, encouraging and re-freshing to confess the six words regularly, of-ten 2 or 3 times a week. They are still my focusing declarations.

3/ On my daily walk/run, I try to add, to speak out other Scriptures regularly, at least once a week.

4/ On my daily walk/run, I am not seeking some mystical and solitary transfiguration. Rather, I seek to enjoy the Lord and the experience, including interaction with neighbors.

5/ Confessing God's word is meant to be more sheer de-light than mere duty.

4/ God can also bless silence.

# Journal Note #10:

# Medications and meditations

Let the record show: this Journal Note is on the playful side. Somehow it helps me to connect medication and meditation.

Maybe because I have to deal with both of these "med" words every single day.

Anyway, my thoughts go back several decades to a Sunday morning church bulletin. Hundreds of us scanned the "Order of Worship," there to behold, halfway down on the left side, these words: "Moments of Medication." I think those moments came right after the offering. Makes you wonder just what was passing around in those offering plates.

Enough already. The typist just missed it by one letter. She tapped the "c" key instead of the "t".

So let me push the point. Medication and meditation are connected in several ways. Both are intended to improve the quality of our lives. Both require regular doses. And both require a significant investment. One, mostly in money; the other in time and concentration.

Presently incurable diseases like Parkinson's are treatable, with a range of medications, exercise regimens and movement activities like ballroom dancing and non-contact boxing. Add to that healthy eating habits, plenty of rest and enjoyable social contacts.

For treating Parkinson's disease, sinemet is still the "gold standard." It results in the production of synthetic and temporary dopamine, thereby giving some short term relief from typical symptoms like stiffness and slow body movements. In its most affordable form, you take it several times a day. (The more convenient, once-a-day form of the medication is currently several times the cost.)

When you are taking medications, you tend to meditate on desired outcomes and hard-to-answer questions:

> How can I best manage the occasional side effects?
>
> Will the benefits diminish over time, as the experts predict?
>
> Can I find a less expensive, generic equivalent?
>
> Are there any negative drug interactions I need to avoid?
>
> Do any of my current medications conflict with cold and cough medicines I have routinely taken in the past?

> Are we any closer to a cure, or at least to slow-
> ing the progression or reversing PD?

Some of these questions have definitive answers; a few are still in need of clearer clinical evidence. But this I know: If we're not vigilant, our meditation on medication can drift away from hopeful stewardship of our bodies and into a wasteland of negative, undisciplined ruminations.

So I try to meditate this way:

1/ I thank God for gifted researchers and medical practitioners who are delivering some of the best care ever for PD patients (and others).

2/ I thank God that he promises perfect bodies like Jesus' resurrected body - in heaven. Meditate on that awesome certainty for a while. (I realize this is the second time I have mentioned this outrageous assurance from Philippians 3:21, but let's call it just a start in what will surely become an eternal celebration!)

3/ I thank God that we have access to medications that are produced to meet high levels of purity and consistency.

4/ I thank God that there are several, recently available generic forms of standard PD medications. In one case, this brought the cost down by about 80% - saving hundreds of dollars per year. Pleasant thought.

5/ I thank God that medical cures for PD and other neurodegenerative diseases are closer than ever.

6/ I thank God for the privilege of meditating on his goodness and grace, and the inspiration of his presence, an activity that reaches deeper into our souls than even the best chemical interventions ever could.

7/ I thank God that medications and meditation can complement each other.

# Journal Note #11:

# The "Big M"

Here's the thing about mortality:

It is so crazy unpredictable.

One day, you're feeling fine and the next they tell you, "Glad you're feeling fine, but you're not.

Sooo, we want you to take these tests, see.

We'll draw some blood. Several times.

We'll take some samples.

We'll keep in touch.

And - eventually - we'll know what to do. If …

it's OK with you."

And then you hear that other voice again, the voice of Big M: "Hello, this is mortality knocking.

Just wanted to let you know — You and I have another thing to check out. A new thing, an additional thing we just found when we were checking out the first two things.

I didn't say it was fair, and it's way too early to worry, but it's time to checkout a third thing while we continue to process the first two."

That's another thing about mortality: it is relentless in its requirements for attention. Oh sure, you can ignore it for a while. You can delay and feign ignorance or deny it.

But mortality just keeps knocking on the door. And you begin to realize that if you don't let it in and try to make friends, it's just a matter of time — someday, one day, Big M will break the door down and . . .

Take over everything.

So you determine to make friends. And you start by embracing the test-givers and their medical care givers. You remind yourself that knowledge is power and that healing and health are temporary . . . and yet somehow seem today like sublime bestowments.

And then you take a step back, away from the clinical and cynical and empirical to hear from your best friend, the only One in all of human history who totally whupped the Big M and the only one who can guarantee that we join in the permanent solution of resurrected perfection.

> With him!
> And you are lifted! Elated. Re-created.
> > Elevated . . . beyond the
> tentative and the speculative
> and into the punctuated, the truest of the true,
> the place that is forever out of reach from the
> > fleshy and the finite.
> > And slowly,
> > slowly,
> > but with ever-gathering momentum . . .

your very soul is informed
and your heart is inflamed with the trans-
    forming truth, at once earthy and
    celestial:

*"But we have this treasure in jars of clay to
show that this all – surpassing power is from
God not from us."*

(2 Cor. 4:7)

(Written in November, 2015, just before Thanksgiving and just
after another visit to a doctor's office.)

# Journal Note #12:

# PD refresh

When you have PD, it seems like the whole world is getting smaller: smaller handwriting, smaller keystrokes on your computer, smaller steps, smaller voice, even smaller conversations.

It is easy to slide into depression in the face of multiple losses, with no cure yet available.

We all need to be refreshed in the push and pull of ordinary life. But when you are battling PD (or some other formidable foe), you have an intensified need for meaningful refreshment at the deepest level of your heart and soul, your relationships and your very body.

For PD folks, the daily struggle to button recalcitrant buttons, chase food around your plate (my personal favorite food to chase is wobbly jello), open doors which now seem heavy, tie your shoes, lift your grandkids, sign checks, walk straight, speak audibly and distinctly, order at the drive-thru, and on some days, swing a golf club. . . can wear you down, build frustration and make you feel marginalized in your own home.

Pepsi used to promote its cola drink by promising, "the pause that refreshes." I know, I know – they deliver too much sweet stuff in their beverage, but they may have hit on something important, this phenomenon that we call refreshment.

For the past several years, I have been focusing on seven of the best ways to both get refreshed and bring refreshment to others. I call it "PD refresh." Here's the content:

PD
R elationships
E ncouragment
F aith
R est
E xercise
S ervice to others
H umor

Let's not tire ourselves by belaboring the point, "PD refresh" simply means that …

**R elationships** keep us in touch with each other in ways that take each other into account. Healthy relationships are to the soul what a cool breeze is to a sweaty body.

**E ncouragement** fosters a sense of significance: we matter to one another, and we can say so. I like the simple words of a Japanese proverb that says, "One encouraging word can warm a winter's night."

**F aith** that is credible flows from the integrity, love and truth we find uniquely in Jesus Christ. Who could ever sustain us like he does?

**R est** rescues us from non-stop activity and replenishes - something especially important in managing PD. Short naps and 8 hours a night can work wonders. Or at least help. And, yes, I believe in non-addictive sleeping pills.

**E xercise** may just be one of the very, very best medicines of all. Within the limits approved by your doctor, go to it. For me, that has meant walking (mixed with a little running) about 4 miles a day, 3,000 miles over the last 26+ months.

**S ervice** can protect us from unhealthy self-absorption. We are made to get outside ourselves, whether it is giving time or money or our skills. It could start by reaching out to others who deal with PD.

**H umor** is to PD what a shock absorber is to a car: it really helps to cushion the bumps and manage the bounce. Laughing at ourselves lands a blow against self pity, too. (I sometimes tell people, "If you have a beverage that says 'shake well before serving,' I'm your guy. Put it right here," as I hold up my tremor-tending right hand.)

The Book of Proverbs says that *"... he who refreshes others will himself be refreshed." (11: 25b)*

The apostle Paul wrote to his friend Philemon that *"your love has given me great joy and encouragement, because you, brother, have refreshed the hearts of the saints." (v. 7)*

The word "refresh" means to "give rest" or to "ease." Refreshment: We need it. But we also are alive to give it to others.

# Journal Note #13:

# Fresh snowfall, fresh prayer

February, 2017

12.58pm 21degrees and cloudy

Just back home after walking/running 3.4 miles in 21 degree weather, with a light snow covering the ground.

Lord, by your Spirit's empowerment, I refuse to let PD chill my will or freeze my faith in you.

For me, today's workout (as with most of my workouts), was an exercise in freedom - the freedom to move aggressively against the disease that, by its very shortage of dopamine, always makes it harder to move. How's that for irony - move hard against the disease whose very hallmark is inhibited movement.

That, my friend, is the irony of freedom! In and through God's great grace.

Lord, I give you thanks today for your constant companionship. I know, despite my ebb and flow of emotion, yes, I know that I have never run or walked alone for one single second over these more than 3,000 miles in the dawn, in the dark, in the light. In 15 countries, in nearly 2 dozen airports. At home, on the "mill." In the hallways and through our kitchen-family room-living room-bedroom, at-our-house walking path. I wholeheartedly affirm, receive and believe your promise to be with me always - "even to the end of the age." (Matt 28: 20c) And that includes the end of the hallway walking path.

Just so you know, Diabolo: You may delight in dishing out challenges that attack my body. Disease may inhibit my movement, tone down my voice and diminish my handwriting. But you can't touch my soul, my heart, my life which is wholly sustained and blessed by the One who has defeated you and soon, very soon, will totally destroy you. So take your temporary false glee.

But - just so you know that I know - your insidious taunting is but for a moment and lacks any capacity to inflict any real damage. What, however, is powerfully real is the sustaining hope through my Redeemer who is the exact opposite of you: He is true and faithful and awesome in grace and mercy that saves and flows with sometimes invisible, but always invincible, eternal encouragement.

# Journal Note #14:

# Powerful Paradox

*"Therefore I will boast all the more gladly about my weaknesses, so that Christ's power may rest on me."*

*(2 Corinthians 12: 9b)*

I admit it, Lord.

Some parts of the Bible, I would like to edit. To bring them more in line with my preferences.

My editorial nerve endings always wake up when I come to the 2 Corinthians 12 passage regarding Paul's "thorn in the flesh." To me, it's in the same paradoxical paradigm *as James 1: 2. "Consider it pure joy, my brothers, whenever you face trials of many kinds, because you know that the testing of your faith develops perseverance."*

Forgive me, Lord, but my reaction is almost visceral when it comes to divine blessing of pain, of incurable afflictions and trials.

I know that you know everything about me, including my emotional reactions, but I needed to get this out in words, to own up to it, perhaps in a way similar to David's visceral eruptions as he wrote the Psalms.

Thanks, Lord, for letting me express such cryptic thoughts.

I am turning toward you, not away from you or against you. Your truth – always coupled with grace - trumps my emotion any day. Every day. As I settle into a place of inquisitive trust, I'm more ready than ever to be led and taught by your Holy Spirit.

Through your word.

For my (our) good.

For your glory.

So I come back to 2 Corinthians 12: 7 - 10, and I am listening carefully to the words that the apostle Paul speaks, under your inspiration . . . In humble submission in your presence, I accept your invitation to "Come, let us reason together. "

**"To keep me from becoming conceited because of these surpassingly great revelations ..."** (v. 7a)

- so it's true, Paul and the rest of us easily slip into conceit, and a conceit born of spiritual gifts may be the worst
- if a "thorn" can correct our egos, it may actually save us from catastrophe, right?

**"...there was given me a thorn in my flesh, a messenger of Satan, to torment me."** (v. 7b)

- whatever the "thorn" was, I'm sure it hurt. That's what thorns do.

- whether it was impaired vision or epilepsy or something else, it came from Satan, not from God, and it continued to torment. No fun and no earthly cure.

**"Three times I pleaded with the Lord to take it away from me. But he said to me, 'My grace is sufficient for you…"** (v.8-9a)

- Paul asked three times for your deliverance, Lord. Is there a limit on asking? Not sure.
- it seems clear that you don't ever leave us with nothing, but sometimes instead of taking away the "thorn," you fill us with what you call "sufficient" grace - which I take to mean - enough of your grace to sustain us.

**"…for my power is made perfect in weakness."** (v. 9b)

- so, if we are full of ourselves and confident of our own ability, there's little or no room for the power of God to be in us
- God's power, apparently is demonstrated best through our weakness; makes sense for the Creator to empower his creation (us) in a way that is palpable – "handled, touched and felt."

**"Therefore I will boast all the more gladly about my weaknesses, so that Christ's power may rest on me." (v. 9c)**

- this speaks, in large measure, to why I am writing these "Journal Notes;" It is normal to conceal our weaknesses, which, over time, may compound our anxiety and isolation, feeding the inner conviction of inadequacy
- But like Paul, we may be much healthier if we, within reasonable limits, acknowledge, or make clear, Paul says "boast" about our weaknesses for a purpose: that we are receptive, humbly eager for Christ's power to "work through us."
- Paul had a choice and so do we.
- Lord, here is my thorn, this medically incurable Parkinsons. I'm glad about how you can show your power in my weakness. I am!

**"That is why, for Christ's sake, I delight in weaknesses, and insults, and hardships, persecutions, and difficulties. For when I am weak, then I am strong."** (v.10)

- Are my responses to my weakness going to be purely for my selfish sake, or shall I think carefully about how I respond for his sake, his glory, his call upon me to live and breathe in him, for him?
- "Troubles are real but not permanent," I say with the understanding that such an admission may sound trite, even in my own ears. Still it's true as true can be.
- And if this be so, then the paradox - two seemingly contradictory statements - is not a whiney, wimp-out on reality. The paradox of "when I am weak, then I am

strong" is, in fact, a valid, powerful and inspired statement of God's truth.
- Lord, I yield my emotions, my mind and my will to you and every part of your word – including 2 Corinthians 12: 7-10!

Years ago, a Godly grandfather was visiting his grandchildren who lived in another state. As he caught up with family events, he learned that his 6 year old grandson has recently made a sincere decision to follow Christ.

"Bobby," the grandfather asked, "are you still following Jesus?"

"No," the boy answered quietly.

"Why not?"

"Couldn't live it."

Paul's "thorn-in-the-flesh" declaration we've just walked through in this Journal Note #14, can easily trigger discouragement in adults who, despite cognitive analysis and deep faith, become convinced that it is just impossible to live it.

But if we listen beyond the noise of culture and cynicism and personal culpability, we can hear the distinct voice of the One who says not, "your ego is sufficient," or "your power is all you need."

We hear the voice of the One who affirms: "my grace is sufficient," and "my power will do for you what you can never do for yourself. Try me. Lift up your weakness to me, and as you do, I will take hold of the heavy, unbearable part. And I will never let you go into free-fall."

That's what I hear.

Journal Note #15:

# Five minutes at a time

There's a song I downloaded a while ago that says, "Every day it starts all over again…"

Words like that could go downhill in a hurry, if the song merely took up a protest against the tedium of life, likening us to travelers on a treadmill.

But the songwriters (Daryl Williams and Sheri LaFontaine) chose a different direction. They continue:

> ". . . New mercy with the dawn
> His faithfulness goes on and on . . .
> Everyday it starts all over again
> **Verse 1**
> Great is His faithfulness, mighty are His ways
> Day by day I marvel as I stand back and survey
> Everything I've needed He's there to provide
> Joy returns each morning
> Right before my eyes
> **Verse 2**
> Standing on His promises, trusting in His
> grace

Morning by morning I find a resting place
He's the God of my salvation, the Lord of my
life
His love has no limits, no boundary of time

**Chorus**
Everyday it starts all over again
New mercy with the dawn
His faithfulness goes on and
Gone is all the guilt, the worry of sin
It's all been washed away
Everyday . . ."
(repeat)

The focus is on fresh and refreshed starts every day, reminiscent of Lamentations 3:

*"Yet I will still dare to hope
when I remember this:
The faithful love of the Lord never ends!
. . . His mercies begin afresh each morning."*
*(Lamentations 3: 21-22a, 23b) NLT*

A group called "Three Bridges" recorded "Everyday It Starts All Over Again" on their CD entitled, "Breakin' Chains," released in 2007. I enjoy this group and have a few of their songs on my iphone.

To be honest, I try not to get stuck on any one song for very long. I find that music often sticks in my head longer than spoken words, and I can get dominated by a tune - to excess.

This song, "Everyday it starts all over" is a gem, worth repeating. But no one song can cover all the bases.

I want more than one song to sing; more than one theme to think. And if I am going to obsess, Lord, let me obsess on your majesty and mercy. Help me to enjoy the mix of grand-kids and prayers and exercise and car shopping and sports and worship and preaching and teaching and good food --- five minutes at a time.

What I'm seeking is not superficialty or a denial of my do-pamine deficiency. I am looking to be fully present in the mo-ments of life in all of their splendid variety.

Help me to avoid a sing-songy, vain repetitiousness.

Teach me to walk and run with you, Lord Jesus. Five min-utes at a time for the rest of my life.

You, Lord, are the Master of fullness in what can become an increasingly empty world.

(Sometime later, I added this note to myself: Just so you know, self, your Note #15 sounds a little confusing. What is your point?

My answer is simply this: PD has introduced a new ele-ment of uncertainty to my life. For one thing, PD is neurode-generative - it tends to get worse over time. I know that. But I do not want speculation over future difficulties to overshadow and kill the joy of today. I want to live in God's fullness. To the max. A step at a time. Gladly. Five minutes at a time. Full of hope. . . Yet, without hype.)

# Journal Note #16:

# The tug-of-war with myself

Along the way of putting these "Journal Notes" together, I have had several moments of "buyer's remorse," or at least "writer's second thoughts." In those times, I have aggressively second-guessed my decision to put a spotlight on PD, including my own PD.

Why?

Because as I have shared so many times, "Our diseases do not define us. My PD does not change who I am as a person, no matter if I rasp when I talk or sway when I walk. It's our heart for God and for people that really defines who we are!"

In that light, it's easy to feel uneasy about revealing so much about yourself, seen through the prism of PD.

So why am I doing this?

One. I want to encourage others with PD.

- to not be ashamed; we all have some infirmity of one kind or another

- to laugh and love and live, to the max, always exploring new resources for fighting back against PD
- to receive more fully the blessings of a living faith in Jesus Christ, especially as it relates to the saga of medical incurability
- to reach out to others, expressing personal interest and helpfulness

Two. I want to break down some of the stereotypes regarding PD

- yes, we can live full, active lives
- yes, we can slow and delay many of the symptoms
- yes, PD is primarily a movement disorder; multiple symptoms may emerge, but not inevitably or uniformly

Three. I want to give gratitude and glory to God

- gratitude for the blessings I could not have received without PD opening my heart and mind to God's greater grace and strength
- glory to God for his power to sustain us and ultimately heal us

Four. I want to express the huge difference family and friends can make

- if we accept one another
- as we encourage one another
- when we step up in attentiveness to one another

So, I will take the risk of putting my "Journal Notes" out there . . . believing that I can make at least a modest contribution to the hope, the health and well-being of fellow travelers. Shalom.

# Journal Note #17:

# When clay jars meet their Maker

It is early Sunday afternoon.

I am just home from preaching 3 times this morning - a challenging but always worthwhile workout.

And I'm full. Thanks to Carol and a wonderful Sunday dinner that she prepared. She's a marvel to keep those great meals coming all during the week. In fact, for years of weeks!

But I'm also full of multi-sensory gratitude to God.

Let me see if I can unpack that outburst of mind, body and soul.

Our Scriptural focus this morning was on patience, especially Jesus' assertion that the word of God *"...that fell on the good soil represents honest, good-hearted people who hear God's word, cling to it, and patiently produce a huge harvest."* (Luke 8:15) NLT

This "huge harvest" he promises seems to be evident in our humble, daily obedience to the Lord and our patient follow-through in a life that blesses those around us. If we pay attention and patiently follow-through, we wind up fulfilling our purpose and our potential.

Always, by his grace.

No reason for self-pity here.

I am always stirred, sometimes puzzled and yet profoundly grateful for the credible message of Christ. The way he perfectly combined orthodoxy (right statements) and orthopraxy (right actions) delivers fullness not found elsewhere.

But here's the thing: More than ever, I see in myself (and others) a need for constant refreshment in this life of patient productivity that Jesus speaks about. At times - like this morning - I realize how my voice can decline, and how it is a bit harder to maintain high energy in speaking and I realize how much I need the Lord's refreshment. To be sure, PD has a lot to do with all of this, but I am convinced that the physiological signs are merely outer indicators of my (our) deeper needs.

And I am thankful that PD has made this more clear to me than it ever was pre-PD.

Oh, for a long time I've recognized our body-heart-soul connection. But PD has forced me to depend on the Lord's renewing work within me in order for me to do anything - even speak and walk up and down the stairs to the stage this morning in church.

I feel downright exposed sometimes.

Like a "clay jar" exposed to public inspection.

And I pray that my neurological issues will neither draw too much attention to themselves nor, on the other hand, will I pretend that I float along in a zone of self-congratulatory, mind-over matter, non-stop happy days.

Here's where I pause, because I want to get this right: as nearly as I can describe my state of overall well-being, living with PD . . .

> . . . most of the time, I feel good
> . . . some of the time, I feel great
> . . . and only on rare occasions do I feel "not so hot"

Compared to so many physical afflictions, mine is constant but much more manageable than most.

> Probably my single, most frustrating challenge is speaking clearly and with sufficient volume. Some days, I feel almost back to "normal." But every day, there is at least some extra effort required to cope.

All things considered, I feel greatly challenged but also, greatly blessed!

As I try to navigate this changing season of life, finding fresh hope in the midst of fresh challenges inherent in PD, I am drawn again to the straight talk of the apostle Paul in his second letter to the Corinthians:

> *"But we have this treasure in jars of clay to show that this all-surpassing power is from God and not from us. We are hard pressed on every side, but not crushed; perplexed but not*

*in despair; persecuted, but not abandoned; struck down, but not destroyed."*

*(4: 7-9)*

And I respond:

1/ Lord, I get the "clay" concept of our fragility, but you are still the perfect potter, at work to shape our clay. Right? Right!

2/ Lord, unlike clay, I (we) have choices. I choose confidence in you and desire - in my inmost being - to cooperate with your plans for me (us).

3/ Lord, let my life shout out with overwhelming gladness, "There is absolutely no doubt that your power is beyond shock and awe; it is quite simply more than enough!" Or so it seems to me.

4/ Lord, give me grace to be more impressed by your protection than by the persistent perplexities.

5/ Lord, in the midst of pressures and knock-downs, show us your prevailing, life-preserving hope.

# The "D Factor:" Jesus speaks to the why

As far as we know, Jesus never got sick. The Bible gives us no health record for him, except to say that the young Messiah, *"... grew in wisdom and in stature and in favor with God and all the people." (Luke 2:52)*

And yet, Jesus spent a lot of his 3 year public ministry helping and healing people with physical afflictions - from blindness and leprosy to deafness and what the New Testament calls "the palsy."

His compassion, coupled with absolute power over every physical affliction, is amazing to behold.

One of Jesus' encounters particularly stands out to me:

> *"As he went along, he saw a man blind from birth.*
>
> *His disciples asked him, 'Rabbi, who sinned, this man or his parents, that he was born blind?' Neither this man or his parents*

*sinned', said Jesus, 'but this happened so that the work of God might be displayed in his life.'"*

*(John 9: 1-3)*

One word in this account has always grabbed me - "displayed." Let's call it the "D Factor."

In truth, the "D Factor" is not meant to be tricky or ambiguous. Now I am not an expert in New Testament Greek, but I know that this "D Factor" in the Greek is pretty straightforward. The word translated "displayed" in the English is "phaneroo" in the Greek, and it means, "to render apparent, to manifestly declare, to show outwardly and openly that which has been hidden or unknown."

Jesus' disciples looked for somebody to blame for the man's blindness. Somehow, our twisted pursuit of causation can be temporarily satisfied by assigning blame. So they insisted, "Somebody sinned here. Was it this man or was it his parents?"

I find Jesus' response both disarming and refreshing!

Enough with the blame game.

Who sinned, thereby causing this blindness?

*"Neither this man or his parents ..."* says Jesus.

Our search for meaning in this miracle will have to take another direction now --- away from assigning blame, and toward Jesus' exposure of God's power to deal with our issues.

Here's where my humanity is just as limited as the disciples.

I love the fact that Jesus rapidly healed the blind man in order to display the power of God.

But what if - in our time and space, in our personal afflictions - Jesus chooses not to heal us immediately? What does that display? Where's the "work of God" in that?

Could it be that Jesus is exposing two kinds of displays in our day and time?

One, and our preferred display of God's power, is when he heals us fast, as in the case of the blind man: here's mud in your eye, go wash yourself, come back seeing. Praise God!

But there is also a two:

We bring our affliction to Jesus and he decides to lead us, to help us, to display his power by taking us through it rather than out of it.

It takes faith in him, either way.

But it actually may take deeper faith to trust him in the midst of affliction, as he gives grace to cope, than to watch him take away the affliction.

Let us pray, I say. But not with glibness or snappy answers.

I find this prayer comes more slowly and goes something like this:

"Lord Jesus. Rabbi. I love it when you display your authority over every kind of physical affliction. When you heal fast, somehow the power of God goes on display like a bolt of lightning. But I covenant to trust you as fully as I know how - here and now - if you choose to lead me through affliction rather than out of it. I can wait until heaven for the cure, if that will display your glory, your power and your gracious presence."

Is that it?

Yes. For now.

# Journal Note #19:

# Combatants and care-givers: allies in the battle

How well I recall the way our first child pushed for independence.

Scott was strong, so strong that even in his first year he moved incessantly, from jumping up and down on our laps, to pulling himself up on the furniture, to walking. "Early walking," they called it.

One of his favorite toddler phrases was, "Cottie do it! Cottie do it!"

He was a wonder, and he was our first.

We have six children and eight grandchildren now and each of them - in their own ways - have exhibited that same early childhood proclivity to independence. It's natural.

We adults are thoroughly accustomed to walking on our own, buttoning shirts without assistance and speaking without the need for others to repeat or clarify.

When PD kicks in, this begins to change. It can be a chore for men to tie their ties, for women to apply makeup, for us to speak distinctly and loudly enough.

People - sometimes even strangers - try to help. At home, we routinely hear questions like, "Are you ready yet?" or "Can I do that for you?" All because we are moving more slowly and with greater required effort.

This new era of adjustment can be difficult, not just for those of us battling PD, but also for those closest to us. PD literature usually calls them "caregivers."

I prefer to think of them as "caring partners."

Perhaps that distinction reveals my reluctance to accept help.

Maybe.

But more to the point, folks with PD usually want to do as much as they can for themselves as long as they can and as well as they can. They don't want to become a "burden;" they don't want others to speak for them and they don't want to slip into an habituated dependency that reinforces a life of withdrawal.

Reversion to some measure of that early childhood push for independence is probably healthy - at any age or stage of physical health - but especially if you are dealing with PD.

But . . . I tell myself, don't allow your aggression against the disease to spill over into combat with people. In other words, let's not get huffy towards those who try to help. And let's accept that - over time - we may need a graduated increase in assistance.

And for goodness sake, let's appreciate and cherish the constant acts of kindness and helpfulness streaming from those closest to us - our spouses, our children, our grandchildren, our friends, our doctors and related helpers.

As I (we) wrestle with the balance between independence and receiving help where needed, here's some straight talk, offered in love:

For those with PD (or some other relentless foe):

1/ Knock off the grouchy demeanor and be glad somebody cares about you.

2/ Say thanks. Often.

3/ Do all that you can for youself: buy pre-knotted ties; use cuff links if buttoning shirt cuffs is tough; rise up from chairs on your own; cut up your own meat; order you own meal at the restaurant. And the qualifier for all of this is, "if at all possible."

4/ Measure time differently. If it used to take 15 minutes to shower, it may now require 20 or 25 or more.

Stop applying the old standard and celebrate your task completions on your "new normal."

5/ Reward yourself - and your partner/caregiver - with something special from time to time: Have a fresh donut. Enjoy warm chocolate chip cookies with ice cold milk. Slice up a chilled pineapple. Sip a fresh brewed coffee. Take a day trip. Catch a sporting event. (All within the limits of doctor's orders.)

For partners/caregivers:

1/ You are quickly becoming eligible for sainthood.
2/ Keep a sense of humor about your impulse to rescue and "solve it." There's only one Messiah, and he's already been here.
3/ Stay flexible. The needs and the capabilities of your friend may change a bit from day to day.
4/ Guard your friend's dignity. Whatever their shifting limitations may be, they are worthy of your respect and appreciation.
5/ Take time out to enjoy diversion and renewal apart from your friend. No matter how dear or how demanding they are, you both need periodic breaks.

I find myself deeply moved - inspired is more like it - by the growing cadre of courageous PD "combatants" I am getting to know around the country. They fight back valiantly against the disease daily, and they are not alone. They are joined by their partners in the journey who, to one degree or another, give care.

When we ask how they all carry on in the face of what every medical compendium calls an "incurable" disease, the wonder of simple faith often emerges, a faith in the God who protects and assures.

No glossing over the battle.

No false, ego-based bravado.

Just confidence that God will keep his word, as specifically as Isaiah describes God's promise in chapter 40:

*"He gives power to the weak*
*and strength to the powerless.*
*Even youths will become weak and tired,*
*and young men will fall in exhaustion.*
*But those who trust in the Lord will find new*
*strength.*
*They will soar high on wings like eagles.*
*They will run and not grow weary.*
*They will walk and not faint."*

*(Isaiah 40: 29-31)* NLT

It's about confidence that the Lord will protect us from the hopelessness that can drift in all around us, like some poison gas to the soul.

I find myself coming back and rehearsing the realism, the clarity and the absolute assurance of the Lord's protection against lethal attacks in this life, as Paul captures it in his second letter to the Corinthians. (Yes, I know we looked at this Scripture in Note # 17. But, lets breathe in more oxygen for the soul, as we receive it again):

*"We are hard-pressed on every side, but not*
*crushed; perplexed but not in despair; perse-*
*cuted but not abandoned; struck down but not*
*destroyed."*

*(2 Corinthians 4: 8-9)*

O the wonder of such positive negatives! Tough times? Yes. Perplexity? That too.

But . . . we are not crushed, not in despair, not abandoned, not destroyed.

That assurance - from the God of "all-surpassing power" - may just offer the most ultimate care we could ever hope to find, in this life and the next.

It may take a lifetime to fully internalize, but I think that tonight . . . Carol and I will rest in that care.

# Journal Note #20:

# What about "the fam"?

One of my all-time memorable movies is, "What About Bob?"

Bob is, without a doubt, the quintessential neurotic who blithely ingratiates himself to his psychiatrist's family - or "the fam" as Bob likes to call them - much to the consternation of the increasingly marginalized doctor-husband-father.

Like a family pet, Bob proceeds to curry sympathy and preferential treatment, triggering conflict and misunderstanding in the psychiatrist's family at every turn.

With comedic genius, the film exposes the dysfunction of family disunity.

The larger point, not so comical, is that long-term diseases like Parkinsons often put some new and unanticipated pressures on real, non-fictional families.

A major key to coping, even thriving, is PAT - patience and thoughtfulness. And a little knowlege about Parkinsons doesn't hurt either.

I am blessed with a wonderful wife and family who have expressed PAT in so many ways. Here are just a few illustrations of how there is plenty of opportunity for PAT to make a huge, reciprocal difference in families:

1/  PD typically causes a person to speak much more softly and less distinctly. Since these changes are likely to occur slowly, the rest of the family may very well ignore them, unintentionally excluding the PD member from normal conversation.

What the 'fam" ignores, the person with PD cannot. They may feel a growing sense of being "on the outside, looking in" when it comes to family prayer and conversations at the dinner table, interactions with their spouse or children and others. Even answering the phone can become a daunting task, for fear of not having enough clarity and volume.

I am not dramatizing some strange hypothetical here; speaking is often a chore for me, compared to pre-PD days. But I have some choices, and I choose not to become the victim. I can shoot straight, in love, with my family and invite them to both understand and adjust, even as I adjust. Here, in composite form, is how I have tried to trust my family with the evolving speech issue:

"Guys, you know how easy it has been for me to talk all through the years. And you've maybe noticed that PD makes it a little harder now - to talk loudly enough and to speak clearly. It can be frustrating, but Parkinsons makes my jaw and my other speech muscles work slower. All I'm really asking is that you give me a little longer to say things. And that you give me a chance to get into our conversations. Please don't ignore me when it takes me longer to join our conversations. I'm working at raising my volume and I go a tad slower to try to be clear. Inside, my heart and mind are the same as always in my love for you. Thanks for being patient."

And, I might add, just so you know, I am currently in training to become a Shakespearian actor who never needs a microphone and who, in contrast with those stodgy Brits, speaks with a distinctly midwestern American accent.

[ OK. Lighten up.]

2/  Depending on their age and knowledge base, family and friends will have varying levels of insight into PD.

- Most will be supportive and encouraging.
- A few may assume the worst and fear any conversation about PD.
- Someone might swing into a place of denial and say things like, "You don't seem to me like you have an incurable disease; you're just tired."
- Another might expect too much from you, unaware that you may need more rest breaks than you used to need.
- Somebody, family or not, might even get into comparing your current life with your pre-PD days and muse about "how strong and loud you used to be!" (Almost makes you want to respond, "And I remember when you were thin and in shape .")

. . . but no, that sort of response would not be prudent on so many levels.)

PAT can go a long way in these situations. I try to remember that very few people know very much about Parkinsons. They haven't had to.

I also find it helps to let idle or inaccurate comments roll off my back, unless there is obvious opportunity for a constructive chat.

But for sure, whether we ignore or gently correct unhelpful comments, humor can lighten the atmosphere.

So I say, listen up: Will every grown adult (especially over the age of 60) who hasn't changed a bit in the last 20 years, please stand up!

. . . that's what I thought.

3/ About those family meals . . .

PD can present special challenges at meal times. Understandably, finger foods (like chicken strips) are easier to manage than foods requiring spoons, forks and knives. With PD, our eye/hand coordination slows and it becomes harder to execute precise movements so basic to the middle class, American mealtime experience.

Chopsticks only add to the fun!

Fingers and hands under the influence of PD – to one degree or another – require creative adaptation.

For me, a few things about eating have become part of what we'll call the "new and few precious truths:"

- It's awfully hard to eat peas with a fork. Entertaining perhaps, but flat out difficult. And if a tremor cuts loose in the hand that holds the fork, forget it.
- Cutting up pork chops is tougher than cutting up tender roast beef. Both are a challenge, and you can become very hungry during your extended moments of personal meat preparation.
- Try fish. You might have a whole new appreciation.
- It makes a lot of sense to drink soup from a cup rather than spooning it from a bowl. (Unless it is extremely thick and chunky soup.) Trying to guide a watery spoonful of goodness into your mouth with an unsteady hand can be more difficult than landing a private plane in cross-winds.
- Try to look up from your plate now and then, to connect with your loved ones around the table. Only when you take the time to look up do you grasp the intense energy you have been expending on the task of relocating food from your plate and into your mouth.
- PD just makes eating harder, that's all. Take a breather and realize that, no, they haven't all been staring at you during the meal. It just felt that way.

But enough of the over-strategized art of eating under the influence of Parkinsons.

Let's make a deal: as often as we can, as fully as we can, let's just enjoy one another's company, especially during family meals. Let's celebrate that not even incurable stuff can break the bonds that we share.

Amen.

# Who are we anyway?

That, my friend, is a huge question to which I will not give a long answer.

So here goes a short answer . . . As soon as I retrieve two chocolate stripe cookies and a glass of cold milk. (A little sweetness may just give us better perspective.)

◆ ◆ ◆

By some accounts, we are how we look.

- so grab the cosmetics
- invest in cool clothes
- whiten those pearly teeth
- looking good, feeling good

Or we could just go by the numbers. All of us have some key numbers.

- first-born child
- teenager, adolescent
- 30-something millennial

- AARP-eligible senior
- employed in this job for 25 years
- just married or celebrating our 50th

The numbers tell a lot about us but - by themselves - not much about quality of life.

How about our relationships?

- superficial or deepening
- intimate, trusting, marital
- fulfillingly single
- self-absorbed or reciprocal

When we ponder our identity, it's fair to say that we have at least five selves:

- who we think we are
- who other people think we are
- who we think other people think we are
- who we aspire to become
- who we really are, in God's eyes

And - we might add - who we think God thinks we are.

This identity thing can devolve into perpetual navel gazing if we're not careful, so let's take a turn to the practical side.

When life hands us a major challenge like an incurable disease, our identity matters more than ever. At least for a time, who we are comes under assault and requires protection, because . . .

- we are infinitely more than a set of unyielding symptoms
- we are more, much more, than the sum total of a clinical diagnosis
- we are still the same, made-in-God's image, persons of worth

Since my PD diagnosis, I've had a number of times when - just for a moment - I wished so much that I could go back to how things were before my dopamine diminished. I wanted to hit the fast rewind button when . . .

- uncharacteristically for me, it was a struggle to speak clearly; I stumbled over a couple of words and the store clerk looked at me like I was under the influence. I was pretty sure that he didn't want to hear about the substantia nigra region of my brain and how dopamine supply affects the muscles of speech
- I tried to pray with someone and they couldn't hear all my words; I wasn't loud enough
- it was a great day to walk in the sunshine and yet my legs resisted my commands to move quickly enough to qualify for what we call, "brisk."
- I went out to shoot some hoops in the driveway and found that my muscles were not listening to me like they used to in my years of smooth shooting; today it was a struggle.

You get the idea.

Slipping wistfully back into another time and place, glorifying how things used to be, or simple sadness about loss doesn't accomplish much. There is not much point to staring constantly in life's rearview mirror.

That's why I often make it a point to stop by the newborn department when I make hospital visits to adults who have serious illness.

I want to pay attention, to honestly care about illness and pain and disappointment. For others and for myself.

But as I make my way to the hospital "birthing suites" and then on to the glass wall area where all the newborn babies - "red and yellow black and white" - are nestled in their warm basinets, these little ones are, indeed, "precious in his sight" as the song says.

And so are we. Look no further than the life, the message, the death and resurrection of Jesus Christ.

Hope springs eternally and presently because of this fact: we, his children of all ages, are precious in his sight. We are children of hope!

Am I still a person dealing with Parkinson's? Yes, for now. Is it still medically incurable? Yes, at least for now.

And we'll deal with it, by God's grace.

But I'll tell you what I'd rather fix my eyes on: the Lord's supernatural, undefeatable hope.

- A hope that requires patient perseverance on our part. (Not so much a clenched jaw as a grateful heart)

- A hope that is informed and nourished more by our Source than our circumstance.
  (Not so much a short-view as a long view of life)
- A hope that carries with it the authenticity of God's love and grace.
  (Not so much "what" as "who")
- A hope that is both temporal and eternal.
  (Not so much dichotomous as seamless)
- A hope that is personally engaging and encouraging
  (Not so much face-less truth as face-to-face chat)

We are reaching for the sort of hope that the often-afflicted apostle Paul celebrated in his letter to Thessalonian Christ-followers:

> *"May our Lord Jesus Christ himself and God our Father, who loved us and by his grace gave us eternal encouragement and good hope, encourage your hearts and strengthen you in every good deed and word."*
>
> *(2 Thessalonians 2:16-17)*

P.S. The cookies are finished and so are these Journal Notes. For now.

# Journal Note #22:

# No so fast

However . . . before we cross the finish line with this edition of The Dopamine Journals, there's one more thing we need to acknowledge.

In fact, let's make it stronger than simple acknowledgment.

Let's call it a clarifying confession:

It is a temptation we need to confront and defeat, if our hope is to be healthy and sustainable.

So, here's the thing: dealing with huge challenges and incurable diseases can easily lead us into a cocoon of self-absorption, if we're not careful. Getting outside ourselves is all-the-more important in those seasons of struggle, when it would seem attractive to simply pull our emotional blankets up over our heads and take a month-long nap, away from social interaction and, most certainly, away from the front lines of serving others.

Let's concede that when we are up against a formidable issue, it takes a major part of our energy merely to cope day-to-day. But let's also declare that problems are never an excuse to check out, lay back and write off the rest of the world like bad debt.

One thing I am sure about: the One who created us and redeemed us is never caught off guard or by surprise. Just as with Job, he can and will lead us through our toughest times. And unlike Job, we live on this side of the cross and the empty tomb, assured of God's supernatural truth and grace, perfectly expressed in Jesus.

My point is not to pontificate a naive religiosity. It is more about confessing the trustworthiness of our Lord, the Savior, the Shepherd. It is more about celebrating the joy of serving this Jesus and others - even through the vicissitudes of life.

But now, let's get practical again as we consider a few steps that may help us to turn back the stalking enemy of self-absorption, even as we also take practical, constructive steps toward serving others:

1/ Recognize how easy it is for all of us - disease or no disease - to slip into a place of active, compounding self-absorption.

2/ Differentiate between self-care and narcissism. The first is necessary and steward-like; the second is addictive and tends to kill empathy, compassion and concern for others. It is the difference between regularly brushing our teeth and seeking cosmetic dentistry procedures every single day, for the rest of our lives. Healthy care is not the same as obsession.

3/ Practice taking an interest in other people. Think about their challenges and their hopes. Talk with them in reciprocal ways. Avoid any sense of heroic unselfishness. Just enjoy people. As we reach out, we will shed a few pounds of our own emotional heaviness and help to lighten somebody else's burden as well.

4/ Take delight in Jesus' promise to bless us as we become "salt and light" in other people's lives. Salt that adds flavor to life and light that gives direction through all kinds of darkness. (Matthew 5: 13 – 16) To the glory of God.

5/ Don't try too hard. Jesus' amazing advisory on a fruitful life can very well transform us, if we take him up on his invitation to connect with us. Here's what he said: *"Yes, I am the vine; you are the branches," he said. "Those who remain in me, and I in them, will produce much fruit. For apart from me you can do nothing." (John 15:5)* NLT

But with him, through him, because of him . . . well, it only gets better.

In our daily efforts to cope.

In patiently persevering.

In overcoming.

In celebrating.

And . . . in every effort we make to serve others.

Amen!  (which literally means "Oh Yes!")

# About Parkinsons

**Definition:** Parkinson's disease (PD) belongs to a group of conditions called motor system disorders, which are the result of the loss of dopamine-producing brain cells. The four primary symptoms of PD are tremor, or trembling in hands, arms, legs, jaw, and face; rigidity, or stiffness of the limbs and trunk; bradykinesia, or slowness of movement; and postural instability, or impaired balance and coordination. As these symptoms become more pronounced, patients may have difficulty walking, talking, or completing other simple tasks. PD usually affects people over the age of 60. Early symptoms of PD are subtle and occur gradually. In some people the disease progresses more quickly than in others. As the disease progresses, the shaking, or tremor, which affects the majority of people with PD may begin to interfere with daily activities. Other symptoms may include depression and other emotional changes; difficulty in swallowing, chewing, and speaking; urinary problems or constipation; skin problems; and sleep disruptions.

There are currently no blood or laboratory tests that have been proven to help in diagnosing sporadic PD. Therefore the diagnosis is based on medical history and a neurological examination. The disease can be difficult to diagnose accurately. Doctors may sometimes request brain scans or laboratory tests in order to rule out other diseases.

**Prognosis:** PD is both chronic, meaning it persists over a long period of time, and progressive, meaning its symptoms grow worse over time. Although some people become severely disabled, others experience only minor motor disruptions. Tremor is the major symptom for some individuals, while for others tremor is only a minor complaint and other symptoms are more troublesome. It is currently not possible to predict which symptoms will affect an individual, and the intensity of the symptoms also varies from person to person.

**Treatment:** At present, there is no cure for PD, but a variety of medications provide dramatic relief from the symptoms. Usually, affected individuals are given levodopa combined with carbidopa. Carbidopa delays the conversion of levodopa into dopamine until it reaches the brain. Nerve cells can use levodopa to make dopamine and replenish the brain's dwindling supply. Although levodopa helps at least three-quarters of parkinsonian cases, not all symptoms respond equally to the drug. Bradykinesia and rigidity respond best, while tremor may be only marginally reduced. Problems with balance and other symptoms may not be alleviated at all. Anticholinergics may help control tremor and rigidity.

(National Institute of Health website:
www.ninds.nih.gov)

## Demographics:

- As many as one million Americans live with Parkinson's disease, which is more than the combined number of people diagnosed with multiple sclerosis, muscular dystrophy and Lou Gehrig's disease.
- Approximately 60,000 Americans are diagnosed with Parkinson's disease each year, and this number does not reflect the thousands of cases that go undetected.
- More than 10 million people worldwide are living with Parkinson's disease.
- Incidence of Parkinson's increases with age, but an estimated four percent of people with PD are diagnosed before the age of 50.
- Men are one and a half times more likely to have Parkinson's than women.
- The average age of onset for all people with Parkinson's disease is 60
  (Parkinsons Disease Foundation website:
  pdf.org)

# Helpful Websites

MyParkinson's.org

michaeljfox.org

pdf.org
(Parkinson's Disease Foundation)

parkinson.org
(National Parkinson Foundation)

apdaparkinson.org
(The American Parkinson Disease Association)

mayoclinic.org

# Final Thoughts

I grew up in a wonderful, noisy family of 7 kids. And it almost became 8 as our Mom lobbied to adopt "just one more."

We'll always remember Dad's final response to Mom:

"Now you know, dear, every family has to have a last child sometime." And that turned out to be the last word on the subject.

Well, I suppose, too, that every book has to have a last word, a final thought.

So here's mine:

> I am blessed. We are blessed.
> Blessed, almost beyond belief.

By God's love, grace and hope - given to us through his Son, Jesus Christ.

But take note, Biblical hope is not the same as blind optimism, the willful imagination of something good in the future. Biblical, Christ-empowered hope is the confident expectation that God will fulfill every single one of his promises for those who love him and actively strive to entrust their way to him:

*"For no matter how many promises God has made, they are 'Yes' in Christ. And so through him the "Amen" is spoken by us to the glory of God." (2 Corinthians 1:20)*

Now that is hope with substance! (And - as we know - the "Amen" spoken by us literally means, "Oh yes!")

Nobody has to believe this. Everyone gets to choose their guide, their path through life - be it a person, a philosophy, a tradition . . . or something else.

But nobody is the equal of Jesus Christ, in:

> His truthfulness, both verbal and behavioral.
> His integrity of purpose.
> His sinlessness.
> His sacrificial death and supernatural resurrection.

Who else can forgive, heal and liberate us like he can?

And in our moments of acute need, when we face aggressive foes like disease, disaster and death, we are invited to respond to Jesus as did Peter in a pivotal moment of choice. John records the interchange:

> *"From this time many of his [Jesus'] disciples turned back and no longer followed him.*
> *'You do not want to leave too, do you?' Jesus asked the Twelve.*
> *Simon Peter answered him, 'Lord to whom shall we go? You have the words of eternal life.*

*We believe and know you are the Holy One of
God.'"*

*(John 6: 66 - 69)* NLT

For the Believer, that eternal life in Jesus starts now!

Where, in whom, will you find your ultimate, life-giving
hope?

Special thanks to:
Carol,
my soul mate for more than 50 years, and the one
who has heard more versions of this book than anyone
should have to process in a lifetime;

Dr. Jay Burke,
my neurologist and friend;

our Wednesday night "PD refresh" group;

and Doug Burch,
my first PD fellow traveler.

Made in the USA
Lexington, KY
08 July 2017